HOW DUCKS GROW UP

Linda Bozzo

E **Enslow Publishing**
101 W. 23rd Street
Suite 240
New York, NY 10011
USA

enslow.com

WORDS TO KNOW

brood A group of baby birds all born at the same time to the same mother.

clutch A group of eggs laid at about the same time.

down Soft fluffy fuzz beneath a duck's feathers.

drake A male duck.

duckling A baby duck.

hen A female duck.

mating Coming together to have babies.

oil gland An organ near a duck's tail that makes oil.

predators Animals that kill and eat other animals to live.

CONTENTS

WORDS TO KNOW 2

DUCKS ARE BIRDS 4

A PERFECT NEST 6

LAYING EGGS 8

A SITTING HEN 10

PEEPING EGGS 12

WHAT A BROOD! 14

SWIMMING SAFELY 16

FINDING FOOD 18

PROTECTING FROM PREDATORS 20

ON ITS OWN 22

LEARN MORE 24

INDEX 24

DUCKS ARE BIRDS

Like all birds, ducks lay eggs. A baby duck is called a duckling. A male duck is called a drake. A mother hen welcomes her ducklings into the world.

Ducks are related to geese and swans.

A group of ducklings surround their mother hen.

5

A PERFECT NEST

After mating with a drake, a hen will find a perfect spot to build a nest. She lines the nest with her own warm down. She might also use grass, mud, twigs, leaves, and reeds.

A mallard hen uses twigs to build her nest.

FAST FACT

A hen will sometimes build her nest in the hole of a tree.

LAYING EGGS

A hen lays one egg a day. She lays around 12 eggs in total. Her group of eggs is called a clutch. The color of her eggs depends on what kind of duck she is. The shells could be white, blue, green, brown, or gray.

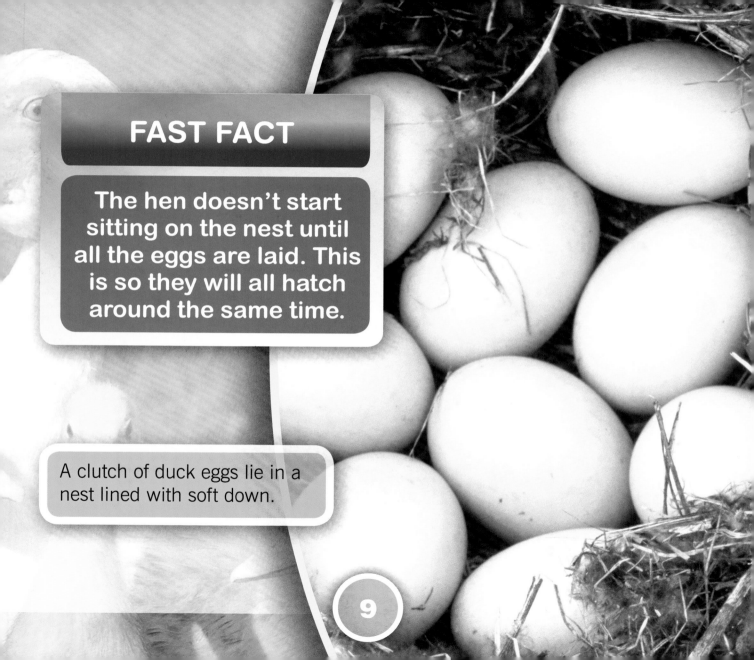

The hen doesn't start sitting on the nest until all the eggs are laid. This is so they will all hatch around the same time.

A clutch of duck eggs lie in a nest lined with soft down.

A SITTING HEN

After a hen lays her eggs, she sits on them. This keeps them warm and safe. She protects them for 28 days. That's nearly a whole month!

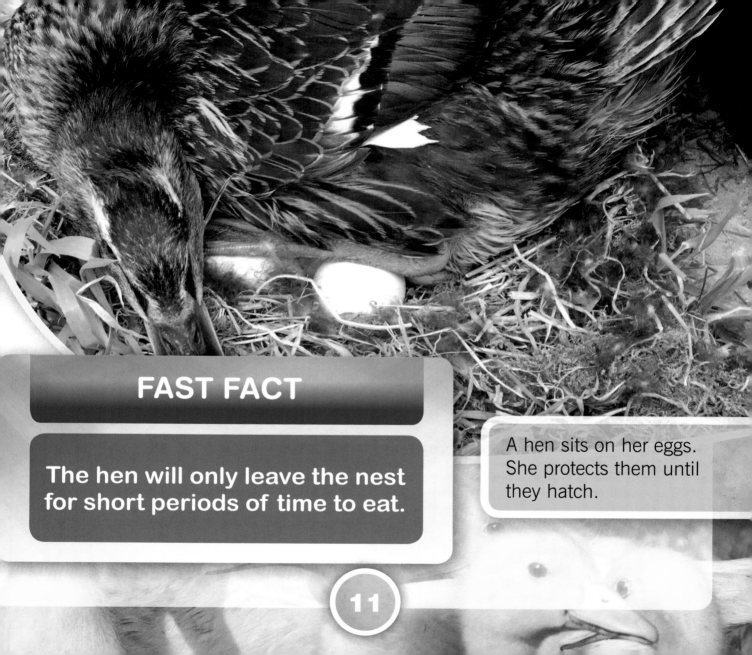

11

FAST FACT

The hen will only leave the nest for short periods of time to eat.

A hen sits on her eggs. She protects them until they hatch.

PEEPING EGGS

A couple of days before the eggs are ready to hatch, small cracks begin to appear. Peeping sounds can be heard coming from inside the eggs.

FAST FACT

Duck eggshells have tiny holes that let the egg breathe.

A duckling breaks out of its egg and rests.

WHAT A BROOD!

All the ducklings will hatch from their eggs within 24 hours of each other. This group of ducklings is called a brood. The ducklings are born with their eyes open!

FAST FACT

Ducklings use a small, sharp bump on their bills to crack open their eggs. This is called an egg tooth. The egg tooth falls off soon after hatching.

A duckling's egg tooth is on the tip of its bill.

SWIMMING SAFELY

A duckling is not born with a working **oil gland**. The hen must spread her own oil on her ducklings so they can safely swim. She leads her brood to water for swimming and feeding.

FAST FACT

Ducks have an oil gland at the top of their tails. They spread oil around all their feathers. The oil keeps the feathers from becoming wet and heavy.

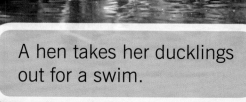

A hen takes her ducklings out for a swim.

17

FINDING FOOD

Ducklings can feed themselves. They will eat grass, plants growing in water, seeds, small insects, and any other food they can find.

A duckling eats a bit of food it found on a beach.

FAST FACT

Ducklings must swim near their mother until they are fully grown.

PROTECTING FROM PREDATORS

The hen keeps her ducklings close together to protect them from predators. Animals such as foxes, turtles, hawks, and snakes eat ducklings.

FAST FACT

Ducklings are not able to fly away or swim fast enough to escape predators.

Ducklings stay close to their mother as they walk. Staying in a group keeps them safe.

21

ON ITS OWN

After about 60 days, a duckling is able to fly. It can swim on its own. The duckling is ready to leave the protection of its mother hen.

A young duck takes flight. It can now live on its own.

FAST FACT

Ducks live in nearly every river, lake, pond, and ocean in the world. The only place ducks aren't found is in Antarctica, the coldest place on Earth.

LEARN MORE

Books

Hasselius, Michelle. *Ducks*. North Mankato, MN: Capstone Press, 2017.

Riggs, Kate. *Ducks*. Mankato, MN: Creative Education, 2018.

Szymanski, Jennifer. *Ducks*. Washington, DC: National Geographic Kids, 2018.

Websites

National Geographic Kids: Mallard Duck
kids.nationalgeographic.com/animals/mallard-duck/
Learn about mallard ducks.

San Diego Zoo Kids: Arctic Ducks
kids.sandiegozoo.org/videos/arctic-ducks
Meet some special ducks and learn how they keep warm!

INDEX

brood, 14

clutch, 8

down, 6

drake, 4, 6

eggs, 4, 8, 9, 10, 12, 13, 14, 15

egg tooth, 15

flying, 21, 22

food, 18

hatching, 9, 12, 14

hen, 4, 6, 7, 9, 10, 11, 16, 20, 22

mating, 6

nest, 6, 7, 9, 11

oil gland, 16, 17

predators, 20, 21

swimming, 16, 19, 21

where ducks live, 23

Published in 2020 by Enslow Publishing, LLC.
101 W. 23rd Street, Suite 240, New York, NY 10011

Copyright © 2020 by Enslow Publishing, LLC

Library of Congress Cataloging-in-Publication Data

Names: Bozzo, Linda, author.
Title: How ducks grow up / Linda Bozzo.
Description: New York: Enslow Publishing, 2020. | Series: Animals growing up | Audience: K to Grade 3. | Includes bibliographical references and index.
Identifiers: LCCN 2018043575| ISBN 9781978507203 (library bound) | ISBN 9781978508224 (paperback) | ISBN 9781978508231 (6 pack)
Subjects: LCSH: Ducks—Development—Juvenile literature. | Ducklings—Juvenile literature.
Classification: LCC QL696.A52 B69 2020 | DDC 598.4/1—dc23
LC record available at https://lccn.loc.gov/2018043575
Printed in the United States of America

To Our Readers: We have done our best to make sure all websites in this book were active and appropriate when we went to press. However, the author and the publisher have no control over and assume no liability for the material available on those websites or on any websites they may link to. Any comments or suggestions can be sent by email to customerservice@enslow.com.

Photo Credits: Cover, p. 1 Jaya Nair/Shutterstock.com; interior pp. 4–23 (background), 5 gkphoto.it/Shutterstock.com; p. 7 Howard Marsh/Shutterstock.com; p. 9 Gary Murray/All Canada Photos/Getty Images; p. 11 Rammkah/Shutterstock.com; p. 13 Anneka/Shutterstock.com; p. 15 Digital Zoo/DigitalVision/Getty Images; p. 17 Edwin Butter/Shutterstock.com; p. 19 Gary_Ellis_Photograph/Shutterstock.com; p. 21 Ross Gordon Henry/Shutterstock.com; p. 23 SkyImages/Shutterstock.com; back cover and additional interior pages background graphic 13Imagery/Shutterstock.com.